KT-405-530

CHRISTIAN
Prayer and Worship

Martin Ganeri/Anita Ganeri

CHESHIRE
LIBRARIES
23 JUN 2006

RL

W
FRANKLIN WATTS
LONDON•SYDNEY

First published in 2006 by
Franklin Watts
338 Euston Road
London NW1 3BH

Franklin Watts Australia
Hachette Children's Books
Level 17/207 Kent Street
Sydney NSW 2000

Copyright © Franklin Watts 2006

Editor: Rachel Cooke
Design: Joelle Wheelwright
Picture research: Diana Morris

Acknowledgements: Baldev/Corbis: 27. Bildagentur-online/ArkReligion: 22.
Igor Burgandinov/ArkReligion: 5, 17. Geri Engberg/Image Works/Topfoto: 15.
Chris Fairclough/Franklin Watts: 9. Paul Gapper/World Religions Photo
Library: front cover c, 26. Spencer Grant/ArkReligion: 24, 25. Christine
Osborne/World Religions Photo Library: 19, 28. Picturepoint/Topfoto: 6.
Helene Rogers/ArkReligion: front cover b, 4, 7, 8, 10, 11, 13, 18, 20, 21, 23, 29.
Brian Seed/ArkReligion: 16. Sean Sprague/Image Works/Topfoto: 12. World
Religions Photo Library: 14.

Every attempt has been made to clear copyright. Should there be any
inadvertent omission please apply to the publisher for rectification.

A CIP catalogue record for this book is available from
the British Library.

Dewey Decimal Classification Number: 230

ISBN-10: 0-7496-5934-3
ISBN-13: 978-0-7496-5934-9

Printed in China

Contents

The prayers in this book were chosen by Father Martin Ganeri. He is a Roman Catholic Priest and member of the Order of Preachers (Dominicans). He is currently the Catholic Chaplain to the University of Edinburgh.

The prayers in this book are a representative selection of common prayers in the Christian tradition. Some of them Christians know by heart and use every day. Some are part of the services and celebrations which mark out Christian worship.

About Christianity

Christians are followers of a religion called Christianity, one of the largest in the world. Christianity began in the Middle East about 2,000 years ago. There are many different groups of Christians but most share the same key beliefs. The three largest groups are the Roman Catholics, Protestants and Orthodox Christians.

Christian beliefs

Christians follow the teachings of a man called Jesus. They call him 'Christ' which means 'someone chosen by God'. Christians believe that Jesus was the Son of God who took on human form in order to save people from their sins. During his life on Earth, Jesus taught people about God's love for them and showed them how to live according to God's wishes.

This stained glass window shows Jesus being crucified on a cross.

Christians believe that Jesus died by being crucified, but that he came back to life again. His Resurrection shows that death is not the end but the start of a new life with God.

4

Christians around the world

After Jesus's death, his followers spread his teachings far and wide. Today, there are more than 2,000 million Christians, living all over the world. In Europe, North and South America, Christianity is the main religion. Christianity is also growing very fast in other parts of the world, such as Africa.

↑ *Orthodox Christians celebrate*
Christmas in a church in Russia.

I believe in God,
the Father almighty,
creator of heaven and Earth.
I believe in Jesus Christ,
his only Son, our Lord.
He was conceived by the power
of the Holy Spirit
and born of the Virgin Mary.
He suffered under Pontius Pilate,
was crucified, died and was buried.
He descended to the dead.
On the third day he rose again.
He ascended into heaven,
and is seated at the right hand
of the Father.
He will come again to judge the
living and the dead.
I believe in the Holy Spirit,
the holy catholic Church,
the communion of saints,
the forgiveness of sins,
the resurrection of the body,
and the life everlasting. Amen

About this prayer

This ancient prayer is called the Apostles' Creed ('creed' means 'I believe'). This prayer expresses what Christians believe about God. Many Christians know this prayer by heart. They recite it when they pray on their own or at services in church. The more often Christians say the prayer, the more open they become to its teachings.

Christian Prayer and Worship

Christians have many ways of worshipping God. On Sundays, and other special occasions, many Christians go to church. They meet other Christians to take part in a service that includes prayers, hymns, readings from the Bible and a sermon. Christians also pray at home as a family, or in private by themselves.

This 14th-century Bible illustration shows Jesus teaching his followers about prayer.

Saying prayers

Prayer is very important for Christians as a means of talking and listening to God. It is something Jesus taught them to do. Christians believe that, when they pray, they raise their minds and hearts to God. In their prayers, Christians thank and praise God for the gifts of the world and for human life. They say sorry for their wrong-doings and ask God to help them to love him and each other more. Sometimes they ask for God to help those who are sick or unhappy.

How Christians pray

When Christians pray, they often bow their heads and put their hands together to show respect. They may stand, sit or kneel to pray. Some Christians stand during church services when they say important prayers, such as the Apostles' Creed (see page 5) or when passages from the Bible are read. Kneeling to pray is another way of showing respect.

At the end of a prayer, Christians usually say 'Amen'. This is a Hebrew word which means 'Let it be so'. By saying 'Amen', Christians show that they agree with and accept the prayer that has just been said.

A Christian girl says her prayers.

Our Father,
who art in heaven,
hallowed be they name.
Thy kingdom come.
Thy will be done on Earth
as it is in heaven.
Give us this day our daily bread,
and forgive us our trespasses,
as we forgive those who trespass
against us,
and lead us not into temptation,
but deliver us from evil. Amen

About this prayer
This prayer is called the Lord's Prayer and it is one of the most important prayers Christians have. It is based on the prayer which Jesus taught to his disciples as an example of how they should pray. In this prayer, Christians call God their father. They believe that God cares about them like a father who loves his children. Christians say this prayer in private and at every church service. They ask God to save them from everything that prevents them from loving God and each other.

The Bible

The Bible is the name that Christians give to their scriptures. They believe that the Bible is the word of God and that God inspired the writers of the books of the Bible to teach what God wanted people to know about himself and how he wanted them to live. Readings and prayers from the Bible play an important part in Christian worship.

A mother in Korea reads the Bible to her children. People are often given a Bible when they are baptised or confirmed.

About the Bible

The Bible is a collection of books, divided into two parts called the Old Testament and the New Testament. For Christians, the New Testament is the most important part of the Bible. It includes four books, called the Gospels (of Matthew, Mark, Luke and John), which record Jesus's life and teachings. The New Testament also includes letters and writings by other early Christians which talk about the life of the early Church.

The kingdom of heaven is like a mustard seed, which a man took and sowed in his field.
A mustard seed is the smallest of all seeds,
but when it has grown, it is the greatest of herbs and becomes a tree,
big enough for the birds of the air to come and make their nests in its branches.
(Matthew 13: 31-32)

About this reading

This passage comes from the Gospel of St Matthew. It is called a parable which means a comparison. Jesus often used parables to teach his followers about God, comparing the everyday life people knew to God's relationship with them. In this parable, Jesus taught that people may not at first notice the power and love of God within themselves. But, like the mustard seed, this power and love will grow if people do God's will.

Bible readings

Christians hear the Bible read out aloud when they go to pray in a church. Readings from the Bible are a very important part of any service because Christians believe that, through these readings, God is speaking to them. Readings are often followed by a short talk by the priest or minister in which the meaning of a passage is explained. Many Christians also read their Bibles at home to help them to pray and to learn more about God and how to lead their lives. Some Christians meet to read and discuss verses from the Bible.

A minister reads from the Bible and then explains its significance.

Worship in a Church

As part of worship, most Christians go to a church to take part in a service. Some churches hold services every day but the main services are on Sundays, when Christians remember and celebrate Jesus's Resurrection. Christians believe that it is important to meet in a group to pray and worship together with other Christians. But they may also visit a church at other times to pray or think quietly by themselves.

This simple church is on the island of Mauritius.

In the name of the Father, and of the Son and of the Holy Spirit.

About this prayer

When they begin to pray, many Christians make the sign of the cross and recite these words. By making the sign of the cross, they remind themselves that the death of Jesus showed God's love for the world. The words they say show their belief that there is only one God but that God can be known in three ways. God is the Father, who made and cares for the world; God is the Son, who came to Earth as Jesus; and God is the Holy Spirit, meaning the power of God which is always at work in the world. These three ways of knowing God are called the Holy Trinity.

Inside a church

All Christian churches are different. Some are very plain inside, while others have many decorations. But the most important part of most churches is the altar, a special, raised table made from wood or stone. In some churches, the altar is called the Communion table. A cross, which is the symbol of Jesus, flowers, candles and a copy of the Bible may be placed on the altar. The altar is the focus for the Eucharist, the most important Christian service (see page 12). Christians sit facing the altar when they worship together. Some Christians bow before the altar to show respect as they enter a church.

This elaborate altar is inside St John's Cathedral in Tiruvalla, southern India.

Sunday worship

Sunday is the weekly day of worship for Christians. They remember that Jesus rose from the dead on a Sunday. A number of different services take place in churches. For many Christians the most important service is the Eucharist. It is also called the Mass or Holy Communion.

The Eucharist

On the night before Jesus died, he shared his last meal with his disciples. This meal is called the Last Supper. Jesus took some bread and wine and gave thanks to God. He blessed the bread and wine, and shared them with his friends. He told the disciples that the bread was like his body and the wine was like his blood. They should remember him in future whenever they ate bread or drank wine.

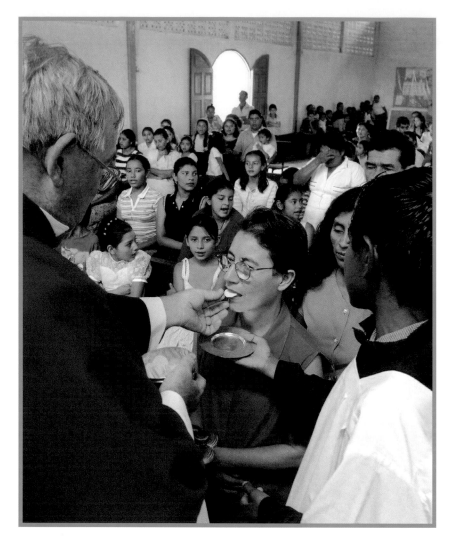

A priest gives bread to a worshipper during the Eucharist.

Remembering Jesus

During the Eucharist, Christians remember the Last Supper. The service is led by a priest or minister who represents Jesus. In the first part of the service, Christians listen to readings from the Bible. Next, the priest remembers the events of Jesus's death and Resurrection. He takes some bread and wine, and calls on the Holy Spirit to make them sacred. Worshippers then come forward to share in this holy food.

The Lord is my shepherd; I shall not want.
He makes me to lie down in green pastures,
He leads me beside the still waters,
He restores my soul.
He leads me in the paths of righteousness
For his name's sake.
Though I walk through the valley of
The shadow of death,
I will fear no evil. For you are with me,
Your rod and staff they comfort me.
You prepare a table before me in the
Presence of my enemies.
You anoint my head with oil. My cup runs over.
Surely goodness and mercy shall follow me
All the days of my life.
And I will dwell in the house of the Lord for ever.
(Psalm 23)

About this psalm

This beautiful and popular psalm expresses the hope that God will take care of us, especially when life is difficult. In the Bible, God is often described as a shepherd who looks after the sheep who are his people. Jesus called himself the 'good shepherd'. This psalm is often said or sung when someone is dying. It expresses the wish that God will comfort the dying person as they face death and that God will take the person to heaven to be with God for ever.

Hymns and psalms

Most church services include special songs, called hymns. Christians sing hymns to praise God and thank him for his great deeds. Psalms are another type of song found in the Book of Psalms in the Old Testament of the Bible. Like hymns, they are used in Christian services and often express praise and thanksgiving. Other psalms express the difficulties or sorrow felt by those praying and call for God's help.

Jesus is often shown as the good shepherd.

Personal Prayers

Christians do not have to go to church or be with anyone else to worship. They can pray to God at any time and anywhere.

Private prayers

In the Bible, Jesus told his disciples to pray in secret. In this way, they could pray to God who sees everything without worrying about what other people thought. Christians often pray in private, opening their hearts to God who they believe sees them as they are. They may use prayers which they have learned by heart or are in prayer books. Often they simply speak to God as they would to each other, or spend time in silence.

God be in my head,
And in my understanding.
God be in my eyes,
And in my looking.
God be in my mouth,
And in my speaking.
God be in my heart,
And in my thinking.
God be at mine end,
And at my departing.

About this prayer

In private prayers, Christians sometimes ask God for help in times of need. Sometimes, they simply spend time with God, enjoying God's company, as they might do with family or friends. Christians believe that God is always present in every moment of their lives, watching over their every action. This 16th-century prayer is sometimes said at night, when it can be a comfort and a reminder that God is close by. Christians believe God is with them every day and every night and will be with them when they die.

A woman says a private prayer.

14

Thank you, God in heaven
For a day begun.
Thank you for the breezes,
Thank you for the sun.
For this time of gladness,
For our work and play,
Thank you, God in heaven,
For another day.

About this prayer

This is a traditional child's prayer to be said before going to sleep. God is the creator of all people, and watches over them at all times. God has made the universe in all its variety and beauty and each day Christians give thanks for the gift of the world and of their own lives.

Learning to pray

Christian children learn to pray at home, at church or at school. They are encouraged to pray when they get up in the morning and when they go to bed at night. They may learn certain set prayers or make up prayers of their own. They thank God for the gift of life and ask for help to love God and others more dearly. They pray for their parents and families, and for the daily things they need.

A child says prayers at bedtime.

Festival Prayers

Christians have many festivals throughout the year when they remember the events of Jesus's life and important times of the year. They are also times for Christians to come together and share their beliefs. The two most important Christian festivals are Christmas and Easter. Most Christians go to church to take part in special services and ceremonies.

A choir sings carols in South Africa.

O little town of Bethlehem,
How still we see thee lie!
Above thy deep and
dreamless sleep
The silent stars go by.
Yet, in thy dark streets shineth
The everlasting light.
The hopes and fears of all
the years
Are met in thee tonight.

About this carol

This is a verse from a very popular carol, a special hymn sung at Christmas time. Carols express what Christians believe happens at Christmas and the joy that they feel at this time. In this carol, Christians remember the night when Jesus was born in Bethlehem. Everyone was asleep and nobody noticed the birth of a little child. Yet this baby was the Son of God, born to bring light and hope to the world.

Christmas

On 25 December, Christians celebrate the birth of Jesus more than 2,000 years ago. This is a very joyful time. The four weeks leading up to Christmas are called Advent which means 'the coming'. This is a time for Christians to think about and look forward to the coming of Jesus. Christians usually try to go to church at Christmas and there are often special services. At midnight on Christmas Eve, many churches hold a service called Midnight Mass. On Christmas morning, people listen to readings from the Bible telling the story of Jesus's birth, sing carols and thank God for sending Jesus to Earth.

During Advent, children often perform nativity plays which tell the story of Jesus's birth.

17

Easter

At Easter, Christians remember Jesus's death and celebrate his Resurrection. They believe that these events were a sign of God's love for the world and of God's will to save people from whatever prevents them from loving God and each other. Easter Sunday, the day on which Christians believe that Jesus rose from the dead, is the most important day of the Christian year. At Easter, Christians remember how Jesus gave up his life at the first Easter for the good of everyone. They renew their commitment to God and to lead better lives, following the path that Jesus showed them.

A priest holds the Paschal (Easter) candle.

Rejoice, heavenly powers!
Sing, choirs of angels!
Exult, all creation around
God's throne!
Jesus Christ, our King is risen!
Sound the trumpet of
salvation!

Rejoice, O Earth,
in shining splendour,
Radiant in the brightness
of your King!
Christ has conquered!
Glory fills you!
Darkness vanishes for ever!

About this hymn

These verses are part of an ancient hymn, the Exultet, which is sung at the beginning of a service called the Easter Vigil to celebrate Jesus's Resurrection. 'Exultet' means 'rejoice'. For some Christians, it is the most important service of the year. It is held after dark on the eve of Easter, or at sunrise on Easter Day. A fire is lit outside the church and a large candle, the Paschal candle, is lit from it. The candle is a sign of Jesus, the light of the world. Holding smaller candles, worshippers walk into the church, singing this hymn which fills them with joy because they believe that Jesus's Resurrection frees them from the fear of death.

Harvest Festival

In September or October, many Christians celebrate Harvest Festival. This is a time for thanking God for all the good things that come from the Earth. Churches are decorated with flowers, fruit and loaves of harvest bread. Many hold a harvest supper for worshippers.

People give food at Harvest Festival for those in need.

*We plough the fields, and scatter
The good seed on the land,
But it is fed and watered
By God's almighty hand.
He sends the snow in winter,
The warmth to swell the grain,
The breezes and the sunshine,
And soft, refreshing rain.*

*All good gifts around us
Are sent from heaven above.
Then thank the Lord,
O thank the Lord, for all his love.*

About this hymn
This hymn is sung during Harvest Festival services. At harvest time, Christians thank God for all the good things he provides. Christians believe that God created everything in the world. They believe that the world and everything in it are gifts of God's love. It is God's love that brings the world and everything in it into being and allows them to flourish and grow.

Prayers for Special Occasions

Important occasions in a Christian's life are marked by special ceremonies and services. These are times when Christians come together to pray and to share their beliefs, joys and sorrows. They are also times when people call on God to help them grow in their lives as Christians.

Being baptised

The service held when someone becomes a Christian is called baptism. In most Churches, this service takes place when the person is a baby, although some Churches will only baptise adults. Some close friends or relations are chosen to be the baby's godparents. In church, they and the baby's parents stand near the font, a special basin which contains holy water. The priest or minister asks the godparents to support and look after the child as it grows up in the Christian faith.

A baby is baptised with holy water.

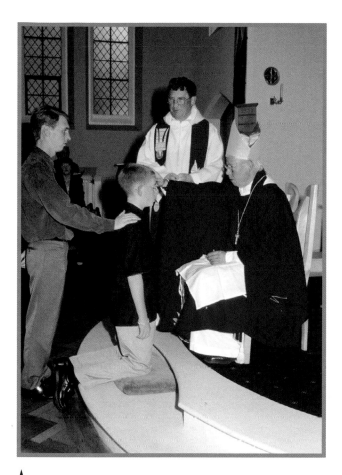

↑ *A bishop confirms a boy.*

Confirming your faith

Another important service is called confirmation. To confirm something means making it firmer or stronger. In this case, people confirm their Christian beliefs. In some Churches, the confirmation service is held when young people are teenagers. Before the service, they attend classes at their local church to learn more about their Christian faith so that they can make a firm commitment to it. During the service, each of them makes promises to follow their faith.

All-powerful God, Father of our Lord Jesus Christ, By water and the Holy Spirit You freed your sons and daughters from sin and gave them new life. Send your Holy Spirit upon them to be their helper and guide. Give them the spirit of wisdom and understanding, the spirit of right judgement and courage, the spirit of knowledge and reverence. Fill them with the spirit of wonder and awe in your presence. We ask this through Christ our Lord. Amen

About this prayer

Confirmation is usually carried out by a bishop. During the service, each of the people being confirmed kneels in front of the bishop. He lays his hands on their head as a sign of blessing and prays for them. In the Roman Catholic Church, this is the prayer he says. He calls on the Holy Spirit to help and guide the person being confirmed so that they find the qualities and strength to live their lives as good Christians.

Getting married

Many Christians choose to get married in church and to ask for God's blessing on their marriage. A priest or minister performs the marriage service. During the service, the couple promise to love and care for each other throughout their lives.

! A couple exchange their vows
↓ at their wedding.

Heavenly Father, source of everlasting love,
Revealed to us in Jesus Christ
And poured into our hearts through your Holy Spirit.
That love which many waters cannot quench.
Neither the floods drown.
That love which is patient and kind, enduring all things without end.

By your blessing, let these rings be to [bride] and [bridegroom]
Symbols to remind them of the covenant made this day
Through the grace in the love of your Son
And in the power of your Spirit.
Amen

About this prayer

These verses are part of the prayers said by the minister in the marriage service of the Anglican Church, as the couple exchange rings. Giving each other a ring is a sign of their commitment to each other. Other prayers ask for God to look after them during their married life. Christians believe that when the couple are married, they become like one person.

Funeral prayers

When a Christian dies, a special funeral service is held. The body of the dead person is taken to church where prayers are said, then it is buried or cremated. During this service, Christians thank God for the life of the dead person and pray that he or she will be welcomed into God's heavenly presence. The funeral service and its prayers help to bring comfort to the dead person's family and friends, and remind them of God's love for them.

↑ *A priest says prayers at a funeral.*

Jesus said, 'I am the resurrection and the life. He who believes in me, though he die, yet shall he live. And whoever lives and believes in me shall never die.'
(John 11: 25-6)

About this reading

This passage comes from the Bible and is read out by the priest or minister at the beginning of the funeral service. Christians do not believe that death is the end of everything. They believe that Jesus's Resurrection shows that they, too, will have a new life with God when they die. Jesus's coming into the world showed that God wanted people to have unending life in friendship with him. The fact that Jesus himself rose from the dead was a sign that God wanted all people to rise again. Christians believe that, through faith in God, they will share in the Resurrection.

Blessings and Graces

In their daily lives, Christians ask God to bless the different things they do and the various things they need and use. By asking for God's blessing, Christians acknowledge and praise God's power and presence in all aspects of their lives.

Blessing meals

Before and after meals, Christians ask for God's blessing and thank God for their food. They say a short prayer of thanksgiving, called a grace. In some Christian homes, the family wait until they have said grace before they start eating. The grace may be a set prayer or a person may make up a few words of their own.

Grace before meals
Bless us, O Lord , and these your gifts Which we are about to receive from your bounty. Through Christ our Lord. Amen

Grace after meals
We give you thanks, almighty God, For all your benefits, Who live and reign, world without end. Amen

About this prayer
Christians believe that God created everything. All the food we eat comes from God, even though people help in preparing it. By saying grace, Christians acknowledge this belief. They also remember that they should share the gifts which God gives and help those who are hungry or in need.

A family says grace.

Blessing a new home

Some Christians ask a priest to come and say a blessing when they move house. This is a good opportunity for gathering together friends and family to share in the joy of a new home. It is also a chance to get to know the neighbours and the local community.

A priest blesses a new home in the USA.

Lord,
Be close to your servants,
Who move into this home
And ask for your blessing.
Be their shelter when they are at home,
Their companion when they are away,
And their welcome guest when they return.
And at last receive them
Into the dwelling place you have prepared for them
In your Father's house,
Where you live for ever and ever. Amen

About this prayer

The blessing of a new home is a chance to give thanks to God and to ask God to look after those who are going to live there. The blessing above reminds Christians that God is not only found in churches but is present everywhere. It also reminds them that a Christian's eventual home will be in heaven with God.

Saints' Days

For all Christians, saints are especially holy people who devoted their lives to serving God. Some Christians pray to the saints for guidance and help in their everyday lives. Each of the saints has a special feast day throughout the year on which he or she is remembered.

What is a saint?

Christians believe that saints are men and women who lived particularly heroic and holy lives, and are models for other Christians to follow. Some of these men and women suffered very badly and were even killed because they would not give up their Christian faith. They were considered so special after their deaths that they were canonised (declared to be saints). Among the first saints were many of Jesus's disciples, including St Peter and St Andrew.

Images of saints are found in Roman Catholic and Orthodox churches.

Praying to saints

Some Christians pray to the saints directly. They ask the saints to pray to God on their behalf, or for particular things they need. They do this because they believe that the saints are in the presence of God but still take an interest in what happens on Earth. Some saints are called patron saints, which means that they look after a particular country or group of people. St George, for example, is the patron saint of England. Some saints have a special interest in helping people with a particular need. For example, St Anthony is the patron saint of lost property. Some Christians pray to him in the hope that he will help them find things that they have lost.

The fruit of Silence is Prayer.
The fruit of Prayer is Faith.
The fruit of Faith is Love.
The fruit of Love is Service.

About this prayer

This prayer was written by Mother Theresa of Calcutta (1910-1997). She was a Catholic nun who worked among the poor and dying in Kolkota (Calcutta), India. She lived a very simple and holy life and cared for all those who needed her help, no matter what religion they belonged to or what was wrong with them. Mother Theresa founded a religious order called the Missionaries of Charity which continues to do the same work all over the world. The Roman Catholic Church is in the process of declaring Mother Theresa to be a saint.

People praying at Mother Theresa's grave, after her beatification by the Pope in 2003. Beatification – declaring someone blessed – is the first step towards making that person a saint.

Prayers for the World

Some Christian prayers ask God for help in solving the many problems facing the world. Among other things, these prayers may ask for God to bring peace to war-torn places or to help people who are hungry, poor or suffering.

The work of this doctor is supported by a Christian charity.

Caring for the world

Christians believe that the world and everything in it are good because God made them out of love. God has given people power over the world but they must take care of God's creation and value it because it was made by God and belongs to God. Christians believe that the world was created for everyone and that we should be willing to share its wealth and resources.

Peace for the world

When Christians talk of peace, they are thinking of much more than the ending of wars and fighting. For Christians, peace means the well-being of everyone and everything in the world. They believe that there is peace when people live according to God's wishes, loving God and each other, and when the world is able to flourish as God intended it to.

For Christians, the dove is a symbol of peace.

Lord, make me an instrument of your peace:
Where there is hatred, let me sow love;
Where there is injury, let me sow pardon;
Where there is doubt, let me sow faith;
Where there is despair, let me give hope;
Where there is darkness, let me give light;
Where there is sadness, let me give joy.

O Divine Master, grant that I may try,
Not to be comforted, but to comfort;
Not to be understood, but to understand;
Not to be loved, but to love.

Because it is in giving that we receive,
It is in forgiving that we are forgiven,
And it is in dying that we are born to eternal life.

About this prayer

This prayer was written by St Francis of Assisi (1182-1226). It shows what peace means to Christians. It is about receiving God's love and being able to show love and care to other people. The opposite of this is what turns people against each other and prevents them from leading full and happy lives. For St Francis, the best way to bring about peace was to put the welfare of other people above his own.

Glossary

Advent The period of time beginning on the fourth Sunday before Christmas. This is a time when Christians prepare to remember Jesus's birth. The word Advent means 'coming'.

Apostles The word apostle means 'one sent out'. The Apostles were Jesus's closest friends and other followers who travelled far and wide teaching people about Christianity.

Baptism A ceremony at which a person becomes a full member of the Christian Church. They are sprinkled with or bathed in water to wash away their sins.

Beatification This is one of the stages in the process which leads to a person becoming a saint in the Roman Catholic Church.

Bishop A leading priest or minister who is responsible for all Church affairs in a particular area. His own church is called a cathedral.

Carols Religious songs, usually sung at Christmas.

Christ A title given to Jesus by his followers. The words Christian and Christianity come from it. Christ means 'chosen' or 'sent by God'.

Confirmation A service held for young people and adults where they confirm (make firmer and stronger) their Christian beliefs.

Cremated When a body is burned to ashes after death.

Crucified Put to death by being nailed to a cross. This is how Jesus died.

Disciples The twelve men chosen by Jesus to be his closest companions and followers.

Eucharist The most important Christian service at which Christians remember Jesus by sharing bread and wine, and celebrate his death and Resurrection. It is also called Mass or Holy Communion.

Gospels The first four books of the New Testament of the Bible which give accounts of Jesus's life and work. The word gospel means 'good news'.

Hebrew The ancient and modern language of Israel and of Jewish people.

Holy Trinity The three ways of seeing God, as God the Father, God the Son and God the Holy Spirit.

Hymns Religious songs which praise God and are sung in church services.

Nativity The story of Jesus's birth which is told at Christmas. Children often take part in nativity plays and act the story out.

New Testament The second section of the Bible, written after Jesus's death, that contains the Gospels and other writings about Jesus and his followers.

Old Testament The first section of the Bible. The texts it contains are

also sacred to the Jewish religion. Jesus was born and brought up a Jew.

Psalms Songs from the Book of Psalms in the Bible which are sung or recited as part of Christian worship.

Resurrection The rising from the dead of Jesus on the third day after he was crucified. For Christians, Jesus's Resurrection gives them hope of everlasting life with God.

Sermon A talk given by a minister or priest as part of a church service.

Sins Another word for wrong-doings.

Further information

Books to read
Religion in Focus: Christianity
Geoff Teece, Franklin Watts 2003

Sacred Texts: the Bible and Christianity
Alan Brown, Evans Brothers 2003

Christian Festivals Through the Year
Anita Ganeri, Franklin Watts 2003

Keystones: Christian Church
Alan Brown and Alison Seaman,
A & C Black 2000

Websites
www.catholic.org
Information for Roman Catholics about their faith, including prayers.

www.cofe.anglican.org
Information about prayer and worship in the Anglican Church.

www.ocf.org
Includes a selection of prayers from the Orthodox Church.

www.worldprayers.org
A collection of prayers from many different faiths and traditions.

Index